CYBER SAFE

A Dog's Guide to Internet Security

By Renee Tarun and Susan Burg

Artwork by Terry LaBan

TABLE of CONTENTS

For my kids, Ryan and Becca—I love you
and may you always stay safe!

To Brett—Thank you for always being my light.

–Renee Tarun

To all my students who are now many ages:

Be safe online and make good choices.
I want you to someday say, "Mrs. Burg taught me a lot . . .
and so did that dog and cat in the Cyber Safe book."

–Susan Burg

Fortinet
899 Kifer Rd.
Sunnyvale, CA 94086

Ordering Information:
For details, contact cybersafe@fortinet.com.

Print ISBN: 978-1-09835-735-1
eBook ISBN: 978-1-09835-736-8

Printed in the United States of America on SFI Certified paper.

First Edition

About the Authors

Renee Tarun is a mom with more than 20 years of experience in cybersecurity. She is the Deputy Chief Information Security Officer (CISO) at Fortinet; before that, she worked at the National Security Agency (NSA).

Susan Burg is a National Board Certified Teacher with 24 years of teaching experience. She loves kids and loves to write; currently, she is working on a series of junior novels about a little girl named Gracie.

Renee and Susan are good friends who share a passion for keeping kids safe online. The characters in the book were inspired by their pets, Lacey and Gabbi, who brought so much joy and happiness to their families. They have left their paw prints on our hearts forever.

Acknowledgments

We want to thank Fortinet for supporting this book and for its deep commitment to cyber safety for kids and grownups alike.

3

WHAT IS THE INTERNET?

The Internet connects computers all over the world. Kids and grownups use it every day!

Lots of surprising things are connected to the Internet!

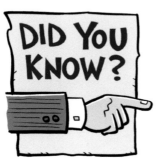

DID YOU KNOW?

Refrigerators

Lights

Cars

Toys

Doorbells

Televisions

OTHER WAYS TO SAY "GOING ON THE INTERNET"

On my phone.

Online.

Watching YouTube.

Emailing my grandma.

WHAT CAN YOU DO on the INTERNET?

Watch videos

Talk with friends and family

Search and explore

Listen to music

Learn almost anything

Play games

Find out what's happening

WHY CYBERSAFETY?

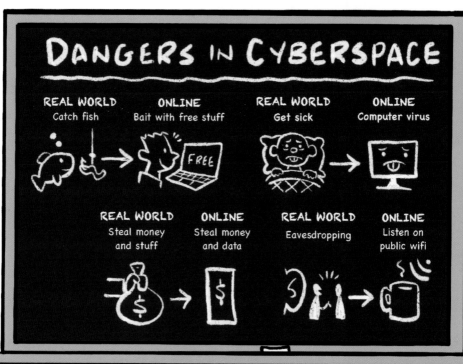

7

PASSWORDS: LOCK THE DOOR!

Did you know? Most criminals use stolen or weak passwords to break into people's accounts.

PASSWORD *Rules*

☑ **PICK A PASSWORD ONLY YOU KNOW**

Don't use your "digits"- birthday, address, age or phone number.

☑ **MAKE IT HARD TO GUESS**
Use upper and lower case letters, numbers and special characters like $, # and %.

☑ **KEEP IT SECRET**

☑ **IF SOMETHING COMES WITH A PASSWORD, CHANGE IT**

☑ **DON'T USE THESE COMMON (AND BAD) PASSWORDS:**

secret	football	password

1234567	QWERTY

ALSO BAD → Using letters as numbers: **f00tball**

And don't use your favorite celebrities, movies, games or cartoon characters!

The best passwords are longer and more complicated.

BAD
fuzzydog82

BETTER
%FuZZyD)G#84!

Always use a passcode to lock tablets and phones.

9

UPDATES AND ANTIVIRUS SOFTWARE

Another way to stay safe is to install updates that fix security problems.

It's taking a long time.

UPDATE 20%

It's worth it, though. Like closing open doors...or plugging mouseholes!

You also have to be careful about free games. Free stuff can come with viruses or malware.

Malware?

Viruses and malware can make computers insecure and spread like germs to other computers.

BE CAREFUL OF:

FREE GAMES

May contain malware or ask for your info.

FREE MUSIC

Free for awhile then your parents have to pay.

FREE STUFF

Usually a trap to collect info.

CONTESTS

WIN!

Many are fake - no one wins and there are no prizes.

MEMBERSHIPS

MEMBER

Clubs are fun but cost a lot.

But I want to play games! What do I do?

Scan them with antivirus software, then play.

DON'T CLICK!

Are there other ways computers get sick?

Yes! Sometimes people try to trick you into clicking on a link or a funny video.

Oh no! I click on those all the time!

Grownups do too. The bad guys keep getting better at fooling people into clicking on things.

STAY SAFE FROM PHISHING

Only open emails from people you know.

If something looks off, ask the person if they sent it.

Don't click on links.

Before opening an attachment (like a picture or a video), scan for viruses.

30%

 Did you know? Phishing means tricking someone into clicking a link that does something bad.

11

DON'T TALK TO STRANGERS

Some strangers pretend to be kids. Online strangers can be as dangerous as real-life strangers.

STRANGER DANGER!

HOW TO STAY SAFE

Only talk to people you know in real life.

Don't share personal information online.

Age 9

Don't confide in strangers or listen to strangers.

Don't ever meet strangers in person.

Don't follow a stranger from one app to another.

If a stranger says don't tell, you should *definitely* tell.

If anything seems weird online, talk to a trusted grownup.

13

POSTING ONLINE

I heard that posting online is like writing on the wall with marker.

Yes. It's easy to do, hard to make it go away...

...and can get you in BIG trouble!

Diego

WHAT KIDS CAN DO

Guard all your info! Never give your name, phone number, email, password, home address, school or your picture without a parent's permission.

Tell a trusted grownup before posting anything online.

BEING A GOOD NEIGHBOR

So if kids say mean things about each other online, it's there forever?

Yes. That's called cyberbullying.

CYBERBULLYING IS A BIG PROBLEM

It's the same as bullying in person, but the bully hides behind a keyboard.

Some people say things online they wouldn't say to your face.

Cyberbullying hurts!

What KIDS can Do

Don't respond to malicious or hurtful posts.	Tell a parent of teacher if you see cyberbullying.	Be polite and respectful to everyone.

When you started talking to me about this, I felt like *never* going online again!

I know. It can seem like a lot of work to stay safe.

But now that you've explained it, I think I can be careful and have fun. Have I shown you that crazy *dog video* I found?

Let's take a look!

15

GLOSSARY

Antivirus
Software that protects computers and devices from viruses and malware.

Bulk email
Junk email sent to many people. May contain viruses or scams. Also known as spam.

Click
To select something on a screen, whether by touch, mouse, keyboard or voice command.

Cyberbullying
Being mean to another person on the Internet.

Cybersafety
Practices for staying safe online.

Cyberspace
Another term for the Internet.

Digits
Personal information like phone numbers, birthdays, addresses and so on.

Eavesdropping
Listening in on other people's conversations.

Internet
A worldwide network of interconnected computers.

Malware
Short for malicious (bad) software. Malware includes adware, viruses, spyware and worms and more.

Online
Going on the Internet.

Passcode
A code or pattern that unlocks a device like a phone or tablet.

Password
A secret sequence of letters, numbers and characters that lets you access software or websites.

Personal info
Includes all details about you, including age, name, address, hair color, birthday, school, grade, teams, hometown and more.

Phishing
An attempt to gather personal information by sending deceptive email or setting up a deceptive website.

Posting
Putting anything online (words, pictures, videos).

Public wifi
Wifi available in public places that is not encrypted (scrambled for privacy).

Stranger
Anyone you don't know.

Updates
The latest features and fixes for computers, devices or applications. Often includes fixes to security problems.

Virus
A computer virus is a program that is designed to spread to other computers, making them vulnerable to attack.

Remember P.A.W.S. to stay Safe!

PROTECT
personal info and don't post without a parent's permission.

ABSOLUTELY
don't meet strangers in person.

WHEN
you see anything sad, uncomfortable or confusing, talk to a trusted grownup.

STAY
positive and don't respond to mean or hurtful posts.

PARENT'S

Talk to your kids

Consider setting boundaries around the following:
- Define how long kids are allowed to be on the computer
- Tell them which sites they are allowed to visit
- Specify software they can use
- Permit activities or tasks that are age appropriate based on their knowledge and maturity

Prioritize privacy

Posting personal information or photos on the Internet can be dangerous, as it can be used by people who want to do harm.
- Once shared, photos and personal info can have haunting effects later.
- It is hard to remove anything once it's in the public domain.
- Check privacy settings on social media sites to prevent strangers from accessing personal information. These settings may not be set properly by default.

Explain the four don'ts:

- Don't give your name, phone number, email address, password, address, school or picture without permission.
- Don't respond to malicious or hurtful posts.
- Don't open emails or attachments from people you don't know.
- Don't get together with anyone you "meet" online.

See something, say something

- Talk to your kids about the dangers of the Internet so they recognize suspicious behavior or activity.
- Let your kids know that if they see something on a website, in an email or in a chat that doesn't seem right or makes them uncomfortable, they can come to you with their questions and concerns.